BATTLE
OF THE
BRAINS

BATTLE OF THE BRAINS

THE SCIENCE BEHIND ANIMAL MINDS

Written by
JOCELYN RISH

Illustrated by
DAVID CREIGHTON-PESTER

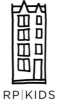

RP | KIDS
PHILADELPHIA

To Kathleen, Rebecca, and Kami:
my clever critique partners who provide brilliant feedback.
—J.R.

For Laurelle, Joel, and Eloise
—D.C.

Running Press Kids
Hachette Book Group
1290 Avenue of the Americas, New York, NY 10104
www.runningpress.com/rpkids | @RP_Kids

Printed in China

First Edition: November 2022

Published by Running Press Kids, an imprint of Perseus Books, LLC, a subsidiary of Hachette Book Group, Inc.
The Running Press Kids name and logo is a trademark of the Hachette Book Group.

The Hachette Speakers Bureau provides a wide range of authors for speaking events.
To find out more, go to www.hachettespeakersbureau.com or call (866) 376-6591.

The publisher is not responsible for websites (or their content) that are not owned by the publisher.

Print book cover and interior design by Marissa Raybuck and Frances J. Soo Ping Chow.

Library of Congress Cataloging-in-Publication Data

Names: Rish, Jocelyn, author. | Creighton-Pester, David, illustrator.
Title: Battle of the brains : the science of animal minds / written by Jocelyn Rish; illustrated by David Creighton-Pester.
Description: First edition. | New York : Running Press Kids, 2022. | Identifiers: LCCN 2022000481 (print) | LCCN 2022000482 (ebook) |
ISBN 9780762479948 (hardcover) | ISBN 9780762479955 (ebook) | ISBN 9780762480104 (ebook) | ISBN 9780762480111 (kindle edition)
Subjects: LCSH: Animal intelligence—Juvenile literature. | Learning in animals—Juvenile literature.
Classification: LCC QL785 .R493 2022 (print) | LCC QL785 (ebook) | DDC 591.5/13—dc23/eng/20220111
LC record available at https://lccn.loc.gov/2022000481
LC ebook record available at https://lccn.loc.gov/2022000482

ISBNs: 978-0-7624-7994-8 (hardcover), 978-0-7624-7995-5 (ebook), 978-0-7624-8010-4 (ebook), 978-0-7624-8011-1 (ebook)

APS

10 9 8 7 6 5 4 3 2 1

WELCOME TO
THE BATTLE OF THE BRAINS!

Birdbrained. Pigheaded. Silly goose. Harebrained. Dingbat.

When humans want to insult the intelligence of another person, they often compare them to an animal.
But animals have amazing brains! And their amazing brains give them awesome abilities.
These various brainpowers evolved to help animals survive in different environments and social situations.
Some animals can use tools, and some can solve complex problems. Some have excellent memories.
A few can even talk to us!

With so many animals possessing such groovy gray matter, the question is:
who has the most marvelous mind of them all?

That's for you to decide because you're the judge in the Battle of the Brains.

As you meet each challenger in this battle and learn about
their brainpower, it's up to you to rate them:

| 🧠 INCREDIBLE INTELLIGENCE | 😀 MAGNIFICENT MIND | 😎 COOL CLEVERNESS | 😕 SOLID SMARTS | 😫 BASIC BRAIN |

You can assign your rating based on whatever factors you think are most important.
Maybe it's the uniqueness of their brainpower. Or the helpfulness of their brainpower.
Or even how loud their brainpower makes you shout, "Wow!" It's up to you!

Once you've judged them all, you will then crown the winner of the Coolest Cranium.

LET THE BATTLE OF THE BRAINS BEGIN!

CHALLENGER

1

THE BRAINY BLABBERMOUTH

INTRODUCING

THE AFRICAN GREY PARROT!

Species: *Psittacus erithacus*

Brain Size: 8.8 grams (a shelled walnut)

Home Turf: The rainforests in western and central Africa

Brainpower: They know what they're talking about.

"Hello." "Pretty bird." "Polly wants a cracker."

When you think about parrots talking, you probably think about one of these familiar phrases from our feathered friends. But African Grey parrots can learn several hundred words. There is an African Grey that sings "Happy Birthday," one who asks Alexa to turn the lights on and off, and another who shouts, "Bombs away!" when pooping.

Extra Intelligence: In Japan, an African Grey got lost and was taken to an animal clinic. He would greet people, sing popular children's songs, and say a name and address. It turned out it was the name and address of his owner, so the clinic was able to find the owner and reunite them.

Even though African Greys say a lot of words, people once assumed they only repeated what they heard without understanding the meaning. However, scientists have shown these birdbrains can actually learn the meaning of words. They taught African Greys the names for colors, shapes, categories, materials, and numbers and then quizzed the birds to see what they knew.

To test identification skills, a scientist held up an object and asked a series of questions related to it. For example, while holding a piece of blue cloth cut in the shape of a triangle:

The scientist asked, "What color?" The parrot correctly answered, "Blue."

The scientist asked, "What matter (material)?" The parrot correctly answered, "Wool."

The scientist asked, "What shape?" The parrot correctly answered, "Three-corner."

To test same-different skills, a scientist held up two green keys, one made of metal and one made of plastic:

The scientist asked, "What's same?" The parrot correctly answered, "Color."

The scientist asked, "What's different?" The parrot correctly answered, "Matter."

To test counting skills, a scientist showed a tray with yellow blocks, red blocks, yellow balls, and red balls and asked: "How many yellow blocks? How many red balls?" The African Grey could count them correctly up to eight!

Since the birds passed their tests with flying colors, it's clear they are not just mindless mimics. African Greys seem to understand words at about the level of a six-year-old child. That's pretty impressive for an animal whose brain is the size of a shelled walnut.

Extra Intelligence: Alex, the first parrot to learn to identify colors, was also the first animal to possibly ask a self-aware question. When placed in front of a mirror, he peered at himself and asked, "What color?" He hadn't been taught the color grey yet. So he saw himself in the mirror and wanted to know more about himself. The scientists quickly taught him the word "grey" so he could answer his own question.

Brain Bonus:

AFRICAN GREYS HAVE GREAT MEMORIES. IN AN EXPERIMENT, UP TO FOUR DIFFERENT COLORED POM-POMS WERE PLACED UNDER CUPS AND SHUFFLED AROUND, AND THEN THE SUBJECT WAS ASKED WHERE A CERTAIN COLOR WAS HIDING. AN AFRICAN GREY COMPETED AGAINST KIDS WHO WERE SIX TO EIGHT YEARS OLD, AND HE DID BETTER THAN ALL OF THEM EVERY TIME. HE ALSO COMPETED AGAINST COLLEGE STUDENTS FROM HARVARD AND DID BETTER THAN THEM 85 PERCENT OF THE TIME. WHAT A SMART BIRDIE!

What do you think about these wordy birds? How would you rate the African Grey parrot in the Battle of the Brains?

INCREDIBLE INTELLIGENCE   MAGNIFICENT MIND   COOL CLEVERNESS   SOLID SMARTS   BASIC BRAIN

INTRODUCING

THE BOTTLENOSE DOLPHIN!

Genus: *Tursiops*

Brain Size: 1600 grams (a pineapple)

Home Turf: The tropical and temperate waters around the world

Brainpower: They like to plan ahead.

Leaping. Flipping. Surfing the waves. Bottlenose dolphins may look like fun-loving fish that are all about playing, but they're actually clever mammals that are all about planning.

Dolphins' favorite plans involve finding delish fish. The methods they use depend on their surroundings, and they often work together. Here are a few of their snacking strategies.

Operation Mud Net: If an area has a muddy bottom, one of the dolphins in a pod swims in a tight circle around a group of fish, using its tail to stir up a giant ring of mud. The fish try to escape by jumping over the mud net but instead land in the mouths of the other dolphins waiting outside of the circle.

Operation Nose-Glove: If an area has **sediment** that is rough and jagged, dolphins break off pieces of cone-shaped sea sponges and slide them onto their noses like a glove. They can then dig with their sponge-covered snouts to find fish hiding in the sand without injuring their noses.

Operation Strand Yourself: In an area with tidal creeks and marshes, dolphins form a line and swim extremely fast toward the shoreline. This creates a wave that shoves fish onto land. The dolphins then launch themselves onto the banks, stranding themselves on the shore. They gobble up as many fish as they can before wriggling and thrashing back into the water.

Operation Trick Your Trainer: At one research facility, dolphins were taught to keep their pools clean by bringing litter to their trainers to exchange for fish. A dolphin named Kelly realized they got the same sized fish no matter how big or small the piece of litter. So if paper landed in her pool, she'd hide it under a rock. Then she'd tear off a small piece to trade for a fish. She'd do this again and again until the paper was gone, earning lots of extra fish. Clever girl!

Extra Intelligence: When you clean your room, do you pick up one thing at a time to put away or do you gather a bunch of things at once to make it go faster? Scientists tested dolphins' planning abilities with a similar task. They set up a box with a fish inside, and if a dolphin placed four weights in the box, it would open to release the fish snack. The weights were scattered around far from the box. The dolphins quickly came up with a strategy to gather multiple weights at one time, so they could get their fish reward faster.

Brain Bonus:

DOLPHINS UNDERSTAND WORDS *AND* SENTENCES. SCIENTISTS TAUGHT THEM HAND SIGNALS FOR OBJECTS (LIKE BALL, FRISBEE, HOOP, SURFBOARD), BODY PARTS (LIKE TAIL, BELLY, MOUTH, PECTORAL FIN), ACTIONS (LIKE FETCH, TOUCH, OVER, SPIT), AND DIRECTIONS (RIGHT, LEFT, BOTTOM, SURFACE). THEN WHEN THE DOLPHINS WERE GIVEN A SEQUENCE OF SIGNS LIKE *LEFT + FRISBEE + TAIL + TOUCH*, THEY KNEW TO GO TOUCH THEIR TAIL TO THE FRISBEE ON THE LEFT. EVEN MORE IMPRESSIVE, THEY UNDERSTOOD THE IMPORTANCE OF WORD ORDER. THEY KNEW THAT *BALL + FETCH + SURFBOARD* MEANT BRING THE BALL TO THE SURFBOARD. WHEREAS *SURFBOARD + FETCH + BALL* MEANT BRING THE SURFBOARD TO THE BALL.

What do you think about these plans for going fishing? How would you rate the bottlenose dolphin in the Battle of the Brains?

INCREDIBLE INTELLIGENCE   MAGNIFICENT MIND   COOL CLEVERNESS   SOLID SMARTS   BASIC BRAIN

3

THE MAGNIFICENT MEMORIZER

INTRODUCING

THE ELEPHANT!

Family: Elephantidae

Brain Size: 5400 grams (a pumpkin)

Home Turf: The grasslands and forests of Africa and Asia

Brainpower: They never forget.

Can you identify each of your friends and family members by the sound of their voice? How about by the smell of their pee?

Elephants have excellent hearing and can detect the call of another elephant from almost a mile away. But it's their magnificent memories that help them recognize who is making the call. If the caller is a close friend or family member, they will return the call and sometimes walk toward it. If it's an elephant they know but aren't close to, they will hold out their ears to listen but otherwise keep doing what they're doing. But if it's a stranger calling, the elephant group becomes **agitated** and huddles close together for protection. Research shows a single elephant can recognize the calls of about 100 other elephants. That's a lot of **pachyderm** pals to remember!

Elephants can also recognize up to thirty family members from the smell of their urine. Since elephants travel in groups that are spread out, they use their extra-long snoots to sniff pee puddles in order to keep track of who's travelling where. Studies confirm elephants still recognize the scent of a family member's urine decades after last seeing them.

Extra Intelligence: In 1999, an elephant named Shirley was brought to The Elephant Sanctuary in Tennessee. As she was introduced to other elephants, the greetings were normal. But when she was introduced to Jenny, they both became extremely excited. They bellowed and trumpeted and tried so hard to get to each other that they bent the bars separating them. Records revealed they had been in a traveling circus together twenty-three years earlier. The old friends seemed delighted to be reunited.

Elephants also have an impressive memory for locations and routes. Their home ranges might be hundreds or even thousands of miles, yet experienced **matriarchs** can lead their group directly to various food and water sources even if it's been years since their last visit.

Brain Bonus:

ELEPHANTS HAVE AN EAR FOR MUSIC. THEY ARE ABLE TO TELL THE DIFFERENCE IN TWELVE TONES ON THE MUSICAL SCALE. THEY CAN ALSO REMEMBER SIMPLE MELODIES AND RECOGNIZE THEM EVEN IF THEY ARE PLAYED ON DIFFERENT INSTRUMENTS AT VARIED SPEEDS AND PITCHES. ELEPHANTS CAN EVEN MAKE THEIR OWN MUSIC BY PLAYING INSTRUMENTS LIKE HARMONICAS, DRUMS, GONGS, XYLOPHONES, AND OF COURSE TRUMPETING WITH THEIR TRUNKS.

What do you think about this trip down memory lane? How would you rate the elephant in the Battle of the Brains?

INCREDIBLE INTELLIGENCE | MAGNIFICENT MIND | COOL CLEVERNESS | SOLID SMARTS | BASIC BRAIN

4

THE INTELLIGENT IMPOSTER

INTRODUCING

THE *PORTIA* JUMPING SPIDER!

Genus: *Portia*

Brain Size: 0.0003 grams (a poppy seed)

Home Turf: The rain forests of Africa, Asia, and Australia

Brainpower: They like to play pretend.

What is a *Portia* jumping spider's favorite food? Other spiders! And when you enjoy snacking on other spiders, you have to be extra careful to make sure you don't accidently become the snack. Fortunately, *Portia* jumping spiders use their tiny brains to come up with tricky tactics to keep themselves safe.

They pretend to be leaves! *Portia* spiders are speckled in several brown colors and have a fringe of hair, so they look like a piece of dead leaf. They also walk in a slow, twitchy motion that makes them look like leaves fluttering in the wind. This helps them sneak up on **prey** and hide from **predators**.

Extra Intelligence: *Portia* spiders can sense the chemical trails of other spiders, so even if another spider is **camouflaged** and holding still so *Portia* can't see it, *Portia* knows it is close by. *Portia* will leap straight into the air, which startles the other spider into moving. *Portia* can then see it and attack.

They pretend to be the wind! A spider can sense another spider's footsteps if it enters its web and will attack the intruder. So *Portia* will wait at the edge of a web until the wind starts to blow. The wind rocks the web, which masks *Portia*'s footsteps as it runs toward the other spider. If the wind stops blowing before it gets to the prey, *Portia* shakes the web with its legs, so it seems like the wind is still blowing. Then *Portia* runs the rest of the way to grab its dinner.

They pretend to be trapped insects! Instead of entering the web of a dangerous spider, *Portia* attempts to lure the other spider out. *Portia* goes to the edge of a web and plucks the silk in a way that mimics an insect caught in the strands. It uses its eight legs and two **palps** to create signals with a variety of speeds and strengths to "sound" like many different types of struggling insects. It's similar to strumming a guitar to play different songs. *Portia* tries different "tunes"—does this spider prefer the Mosquito Melody or the Butterfly Ballad or the Dragonfly Ditty?—until it captures the interest of the spider in the web. The spider approaches, thinking it's about to grab dinner, but then *Portia* lunges and snags *its* dinner instead.

They pretend to be a friendly neighbor! Unlike most jumping spiders, *Portia* spiders also spin their own webs. They will build their web connected to another spider's web. When an insect becomes caught in *Portia*'s web, *Portia* leaves it as bait. The other spider decides to steal the insect and enters *Portia*'s web. At that point, the other spider becomes *Portia*'s lunch. It should have kept its legs to itself!

Brain Bonus:

PORTIA SPIDERS ARE EXCELLENT NAVIGATORS. WHEN THEY SPOT POTENTIAL PREY THAT IS TOO DANGEROUS TO ATTACK FROM THE FRONT, THEY SCAN THE AREA, LOOKING FOR ALTERNATE ROUTES. THEY THEN TAKE WHATEVER PATH HELPS THEM COME FROM BEHIND THE PREY OR DROP ONTO IT FROM ABOVE, EVEN IF IT MEANS WALKING AN HOUR OUT OF THEIR WAY. DURING THE DETOUR, THEY MIGHT COMPLETELY LOSE SIGHT OF THEIR PREY, BUT THEY STILL END UP AT THEIR FINAL DESTINATION.

What do you think about these sneaky spiders? How would you rate the *Portia* jumping spider in the Battle of the Brains?

INCREDIBLE INTELLIGENCE | MAGNIFICENT MIND | COOL CLEVERNESS | SOLID SMARTS | BASIC BRAIN

CHALLENGER

5

THE ASTUTE ANALYZER

INTRODUCING

THE RAT!

Genus: *Rattus*

Brain Size: 2 grams (a raspberry)

Home Turf: The various places where humans live

Brainpower: They think about thinking.

Your teacher asks a question. Do you raise your hand because you know the answer? Or do you slump in your seat hoping you don't get called on because you don't know the answer? This awareness about what you know or don't know is called metacognition. It's basically thinking about thinking, and rats can do it, too.

In one study, scientists gave rats a scent to smell—either cinnamon, thyme, paprika, or coffee. After some time had passed, the scientists presented the rats with all four scent options to have them pick the scent they smelled earlier. If they got it right, they earned a whole piece of cereal. But if they got it wrong, they got nothing. A third option for the rats was to refuse to pick a scent, which earned them one-fourth of a piece of cereal. (Basically, they could say, "I don't know," and still get a reward—although a much smaller one.)

When it came time to take the test, the rats had to think about whether they knew the correct scent or not. A whole piece of cereal was much better than a quarter piece of cereal, so if they were sure they knew the scent, it was better to answer correctly and get the bigger piece. But if they weren't sure about the scent, the rats realized they'd be better off not answering the test to get the smaller piece rather than guessing wrong and getting nothing. The rats' choices showed they were able to recognize if they knew the correct answer or not.

Extra Intelligence: Rats appear to regret when they've made the wrong choice. Scientists played a version of *Let's Make a Deal* with rats. They offered them a reward, and the rats could either eat it or skip it to go to the next reward, taking the chance that the new reward could be something better . . . or something worse. If the new reward was worse than the original, the rats would look behind them, seemingly wishing they'd picked the first reward.

Rats also use what they know to form maps in their brains. If they find something yummy, their brains create a mental map of how they got there by replaying the route in reverse! This backwards playback helps them remember the location. They can later use the info from their various mental maps to imagine the best route from where they are to potential food, basically figuring out a shortcut. Thinking about what you know can be helpful for finding tasty treats!

Brain Bonus:

RATS CAN LEARN TO DRIVE! SCIENTISTS CREATED RAT-SIZED CARS WITH THREE BARS AT THE FRONT USED FOR MOVING AND STEERING. IF A RAT TOUCHED THE BAR IN THE MIDDLE, THE VEHICLE MOVED FORWARD. IF IT TOUCHED THE BARS ON THE RIGHT OR LEFT, THE CAR WOULD TURN IN THOSE DIRECTIONS. AFTER THE SCIENTISTS TRAINED THE RATS TO DRIVE, THE RATS WOULD ZOOM AROUND THE FLOOR STEERING THEMSELVES TO THEIR FOOD REWARDS. ARE YOU READY TO HIT THE ROAD WITH THESE RODENTS?

What do you think about this ability to know what you know? How would you rate the rat in the Battle of the Brains?

😃 INCREDIBLE INTELLIGENCE   😄 MAGNIFICENT MIND   😎 COOL CLEVERNESS   😖 SOLID SMARTS   😠 BASIC BRAIN

CHALLENGER

6

THE CLEVER COMPANION

INTRODUCING

THE DOMESTIC DOG!

Species: *Canis familiaris*

Brain Size: Varies by breed—largest is 120 grams (an orange)

Home Turf: The various places where humans live

Brainpower: They understand humans.

Have you ever accidently dropped food on the floor and then pointed at it for your dog? Your pooch probably followed your finger to the food, happy to clean up your mess.

It might seem like an easy thing, but dogs are one of the few animals that understand human pointing. They are very tuned in to all of our expressions and body language and use what they observe to make decisions.

To test a dog's understanding of pointing, scientists placed a treat under one cup and left the other cups without treats (although they first rubbed *all* the cups with the smell of the treats so the dogs couldn't cheat with their super sniffers). When a dog was brought in, a person pointed to the cup with the treat to see if the dog followed their finger to the food cup. After dogs passed that basic test, scientists mixed things up with all kinds of pointing pop quizzes.

Scientists learned humans don't even have to point with our fingers for dogs to understand. Dogs could follow a point from an elbow or a foot, a nod or a bow toward the treat cup, or even just a glance at the correct cup.

But dogs don't necessarily follow *all* pointing—they also evaluate other clues from the pointing people. In one study, a barrier hid the cups from the dogs' view while the treat was placed, but the dogs could still see the people's faces. While the treat was put under a cup, person A looked at the cups but person B looked away from the cups toward the ceiling. Then the barrier was removed to show the cups to the dog and each person pointed to a different cup. The dogs more often followed the point of person A (who saw where the treat was) rather than person B (who was only guessing). In another study, if one of the pointers had pointed to an empty cup many times in the past, the dogs ignored them and followed the point of the person who always pointed correctly to the treat. Don't try fooling these clever canines.

Extra Intelligence: Studies show dogs also understand our words because the blood flow in their brains is different when they hear a word they know versus a fake made-up word. A special Border Collie named Chaser actually knew the names of 1,022 toys. Tell her to "take Inky," and she'd pick up the stuffed octopus. Tell her to "paw Kiss," and she'd touch the stuffed lips with her paw. Tell her to "nose Never Forget," and she'd touch the stuffed elephant with her nose.

She could also figure out the name of a toy she'd never seen before. Her owner would set out a bunch of toys she knew along with a completely new stuffed cat and say, "Find Meow." Chaser would look at all the toys on the floor and bring back the stuffed cat. And ten minutes later, she still remembered the new stuffed cat was named Meow. Such a good doggie!

Brain Bonus:

DOGS CAN RECOGNIZE HUMAN EMOTIONS. WHEN LOOKING AT PICTURES OF PEOPLE, EVEN IF SHOWN ONLY THE BOTTOM HALF, TOP HALF, OR LEFT HALF OF FACES, DOGS COULD STILL TELL WHICH EXPRESSION WAS ANGRY AND WHICH WAS HAPPY. AND WHEN DOGS SAW PICTURES OF PEOPLE WHO WERE HAPPY, ANGRY, OR SCARED, THEIR HEART RATES WENT UP. DOGS CAN ALSO SNIFF OUT OUR EMOTIONS. WHEN DOGS SMELLED A SAMPLE OF SWEAT FROM SOMEONE WHO WAS SCARED, THEIR HEART RATES WENT UP AND THEY ACTED STRESSED. SO, WHEN WE EXPERIENCE BIG EMOTIONS, THEY FEEL IT, TOO.

What do you think about this ability to figure us out? How would you rate the dog in the Battle of the Brains?

INCREDIBLE INTELLIGENCE | MAGNIFICENT MIND | COOL CLEVERNESS | SOLID SMARTS | BASIC BRAIN

INTRODUCING

THE COMMON RAVEN!

Species: *Corvus corax*

Brain Size: 15.4 grams (a strawberry)

Home Turf: The forests, coastlines, grasslands, and mountainous regions of the Northern Hemisphere

Brainpower: They are good at solving problems.

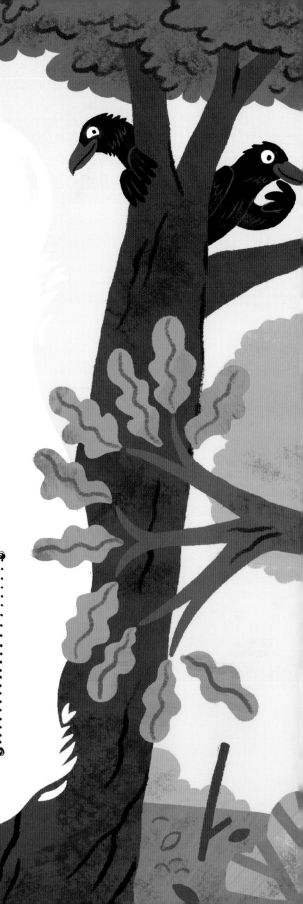

Ravens often symbolize intelligence in mythology and folklore, which makes sense because they have excellent problem-solving skills.

Are thieves trying to steal your lunch? No problem! When ravens find food, they hide some of it to eat later. So ravens often spy on each other to snag an easy meal. But if a raven notices prying eyes while they are stashing their food, they will fake hide it. They pretend to bury it but keep the food in their throat pouch. Then, while the snooping raven tries to steal the food that isn't really there, the other raven hides their goodies in a different hiding place.

Extra Intelligence: The CIA trained ravens to be official spies. In the 1960s, ravens were taught to carry listening devices and place them on window ledges. A human would direct the bird to the correct window using a laser pointer where the raven would drop off the device. The listening device then transmitted the conversations inside the room back to the CIA.

Can't find something for dinner? No problem! Wolves are experts at catching big animals to eat, so ravens wait for them to do all of the hard work. Ravens find wolves and follow them around until they finally go hunting. Once the wolves capture the prey, the ravens swoop in and grab chunks of meat for dinner. It's raven takeout!

Is your snack out of reach? No problem! Scientists ran an experiment where they tied meat to a string hanging from a limb to see if ravens could retrieve it. The ravens figured out that they needed to perch on the limb, use their beak to pull up some string, step on it to hold it in place, pull up some more string, and repeat this sequence until they reached their meaty reward.

Have a tricky math test? No problem! Scientists also tested ravens to see if they understood addition. A scientist put four pieces of food under cup A and three pieces under cup B. Then they lifted the cups for a few seconds to show the ravens the amounts under each cup. Next, the scientist put two more pieces of food on the table for the ravens to see and slid them under cup B, so it now had five pieces. Since the ravens couldn't see the food under the cups, they had to remember and add together the pieces of food in order to pick the cup with the most (cup B!). To make sure they weren't just picking the cup that got extra food, the scientist ran the tests with different amounts, such as six pieces under cup A and one piece under cup B and then adding two pieces to cup B (so cup A still had the most!). The ravens performed well enough to show they have a simple understanding of addition. They are "sum" birds!

Brain Bonus:

RAVENS ARE EXCELLENT MIMICS AND CAN IMITATE ALL KINDS OF SOUNDS: OTHER BIRDS AND ANIMALS, CAR ENGINES, LAUGHTER, AND EVEN FLUSHING TOILETS. THEY CAN ALSO MIMIC HUMAN SPEECH, LEARNING DOZENS OF WORDS.

What do you think about this ability to troubleshoot problems? How would you rate the raven in the Battle of the Brains?

INCREDIBLE INTELLIGENCE MAGNIFICENT MIND COOL CLEVERNESS SOLID SMARTS BASIC BRAIN

CHALLENGER

8

THE LIVELY
LEARNER

INTRODUCING

THE
PIG!

Genus: *Sus*

Brain Size: 170 grams (a pear)

Home Turf: The various places where humans live

Brainpower: They are quick learners.

Sit. Down. Shake. Play dead. Stay. These seem like dog tricks, but pigs can learn all these and more. Performing pigs can dance, play the piano, knock down bowling pins, score soccer goals, and even spell HAM out of plastic letters.

Pigs learn very quickly, especially when tasty treats are involved. People even bring their pet pigs to dog agility classes where the pigs run through tunnels, weave around poles, and hop over tiny hurdles. And in 2018, Joy the pig earned the Guinness World Records title for most tricks by a pig in one minute when she completed thirteen.

Pigs can also learn to be sneaky when food is on the line. Scientists taught smaller pigs where the food would be in a room full of buckets. Then they'd let one of the small pigs into the room with a bigger pig. The big pig soon noticed the small pig knew which bucket the food was in, so instead of looking for the food itself, the big pig would follow the small pig to the correct bucket and push it out of the way to gobble the food. The small pig quickly learned the big pig was going to snag its food, so it stopped immediately going toward the correct bucket. Instead, it would wait until the big pig was walking away or behind a barrier, and then the small pig would hurry to the food and, ahem, pig out.

Extra Intelligence: Not many animals understand mirrors. Only a few species realize it's a reflection rather than a window. However, pigs as young as six weeks old are able to figure out how mirrors work. When they first see their reflection, they grunt and squeal, touch it with their nose, and check behind the mirror like they're looking for the "other" pig. But after a while, the pigs stare straight at the mirror while weaving and making other random movements, as if they're totally checking themselves out.

To test if pigs truly understood mirrors, scientists hid a bowl of food behind a long wooden barrier and placed a mirror so that it reflected the bowl's position. Pigs who had never seen a mirror tried to go behind the mirror to find the reflected food. The pigs with mirror experience instead walked around the barrier to get to the real food. They were able to use the mirror to find the bowl. That'll do, pigs!

Brain Bonus:

PIGS CAN LEARN TO PLAY VIDEO GAMES! SCIENTISTS CREATED A SPECIAL JOYSTICK PIGS COULD MOVE WITH THEIR SNOUTS. THEN THEY TAUGHT PIGS TO MOVE THE CURSOR ON THE SCREEN TO HIT A BLUE TARGET. IF THEY SUCCESSFULLY CRASHED THE CURSOR INTO THE TARGET, THEY LEVELED UP TO A SMALLER TARGET THAT WAS HARDER TO HIT. THEY ALSO GOT A SWEET BONUS FOR EACH HIT—A DELICIOUS FOOD PELLET. NEXT TIME YOU PLAY A VIDEO GAME, GO HOG WILD AND TRY TO PLAY WITH YOUR NOSE.

What do you think about these porky pupils? How would you rate the pig in the Battle of the Brains?

INCREDIBLE INTELLIGENCE   MAGNIFICENT MIND   COOL CLEVERNESS   SOLID SMARTS   BASIC BRAIN

9

THE MANY-HANDED MASTERMIND

INTRODUCING

THE OCTOPUS!

Order: Octopoda

Brain Size: Varies by species—largest is the size of a walnut

Home Turf: The oceans and connected seas

Brainpower: Their arms have a mind of their own.

Imagine that while reading this book, your hand creeps across the counter without your knowledge. A finger brushes something. It tells the finger next to it, "I smell something sweet. What do you think?" That second finger says, "It tastes like a cookie to me. What do you think, third finger?" The third finger says, "Yep, it's chocolate chip, our favorite!" Your fingers snatch the cookie, and you have no idea this is happening until the sweet snack ends up in your mouth.

This is basically what happens with an octopus because it has mini-brains in each of its eight arms!

The brain and nervous system are made of cells called **neurons**. For humans and other **vertebrates**, most of our neurons are in our brains. An octopus, however, has two thirds of its neurons in its arms. These arm-brains are kind of like minions. They can do things on their own without talking to the central brain in the head. If an arm is removed, it will still grab for food and try to put it where its mouth should be. But the head-brain is the boss and usually tells the arms what to do.

The arms also have suckers that run along them. The suckers can touch and grasp, but they can also smell and taste. They send this info back to the neurons in the arms, and since they can bypass the boss brain in the head, these arm-brains and savvy suckers help octopuses react more quickly to grabbing food and escaping predators.

Extra Intelligence: Brainy arms help octopuses manipulate objects around them. They can unscrew jar lids and open childproof pill bottles. They collect rocks to block the door to their dens and carry coconut shells to use as emergency shelters. And they are known for being escape artists, able to undo latches and locks and lift the lids of their aquariums to raid other tanks for midnight snacks.

Brain Bonus:
OCTOPUSES ARE CAMOUFLAGE MASTERS. THEY HAVE SPECIALIZED CELLS UNDER THEIR SKIN THAT CHANGE THEIR COLOR AND SPECIAL MUSCLES THAT CHANGE THEIR TEXTURE. THEY ARE ABLE TO VIEW THEIR SURROUNDINGS AND DECIDE WHAT THEY SHOULD LOOK LIKE IN ORDER TO STAY SAFE. THEN **PRESTO!** IN THE BLINK OF AN EYE, THEY CHANGE THEIR SKIN TO BE BROWN AND BUMPY LIKE SAND, PURPLE AND SPIKY LIKE CORAL, OR GREEN WITH RIDGES LIKE ALGAE. THEN THEY ADD TO THEIR DISGUISE BY WAVING THEIR ARMS OR MOVING ACROSS THE SEA FLOOR IN A WAY THAT MATCHES THEIR CAMOUFLAGE.

What do you think about these brainy arms? How would you rate the octopus in the Battle of the Brains?

INCREDIBLE INTELLIGENCE   MAGNIFICENT MIND   COOL CLEVERNESS   SOLID SMARTS   BASIC BRAIN

10

THE TALENTED TOOLMAKER

INTRODUCING

THE CHIMPANZEE!

Species: *Pan troglodytes*

Brain Size: 384 grams (a papaya)

Home Turf: The rainforests and grasslands of equatorial Africa

Brainpower: They are quite handy.

In 1960, Jane Goodall saw a chimpanzee pluck a piece of grass, poke it into a termite mound, and then put it in his mouth. Turns out he was fishing for tasty termites. This discovery rocked the scientific world because until then everyone thought humans were the only species that used tools. We now know a number of animals (including many in this book) use tools; however, chimps have the largest collection of tools, and they even make some of them. So what are you likely to find in a chimpanzee's toolbox?

Leaves:

Feeling thirsty? Fold a leaf into a cup to drink water. Or crush leaves into a sponge to suck up water from a tree hole.

Is there something gross on your face or body? Use a leaf to wipe it off.

Dealing with a thorny tree? Use a twig full of leaves to protect your hands and feet from poking spines.

Stones:

Can't crack that nut? Use one stone as an **anvil** and the other as a hammer to break it open.

Have an intruder? Throw stones to scare them off.

Sticks:

Want to chow down on some ants without getting bitten? Strip the leaves off a skinny stick and poke it in an ant nest to pull out some yummy ants.

Hankering for some honey but don't want to get stung? Use a big stick to break open a beehive. Then chew on one end of a smaller stick to create a spoon to scoop out the sweet honey.

Craving an algae snack but don't want to go swimming? Find a long stick, pull off the braches to create a pole, and then swirl it around in the water until you've collected a clump of algae to munch.

Chimpanzees can even use multiple tools to complete a task. For example, if after cracking open a nut with stones they still can't get the goodies inside, they will use a small twig to pry it out of the shell. Chimps have definitely learned to use the right tools for the job.

Extra Intelligence: Chimpanzees not only make tools, they also make toys. They play tug-of-war with branches and vines. They toss gourds in the air and catch them. They also use sticks and rocks as dolls. They carry them around, often balanced on their shoulder or back like a baby would be. They sleep with them in their nest, and one chimpanzee even made a separate nest for his stick doll. Sleep tight, little stick.

Brain Bonus:

HOW WOULD YOU LIKE TO PLAY ROCK-PAPER-SCISSORS WITH A CHIMPANZEE? SCIENTISTS HAVE TAUGHT CHIMPANZEES THE RULES: PAPER BEATS ROCK, ROCK BEATS SCISSORS, AND SCISSORS BEATS PAPER. THE CHIMPANZEES ACTUALLY PLAYED WITH SYMBOLS ON A TOUCH SCREEN RATHER THAN MAKING THE SHAPES WITH THEIR HANDS. WHEN SHOWN TWO OF THE SHAPES, THEY COULD CORRECTLY PICK WHICH WOULD WIN 90 PERCENT OF THE TIME, WHICH WAS THE SAME RATE AS FOUR-YEAR-OLD HUMANS. READY TO TAKE ON A CHIMP? ONE, TWO, THREE, SHOOT!

What do you think about this crafty ability? How would you rate the chimpanzee in the Battle of the Brains?

😀 INCREDIBLE INTELLIGENCE · 😄 MAGNIFICENT MIND · 😎 COOL CLEVERNESS · 🙂 SOLID SMARTS · 😕 BASIC BRAIN

AND THE WINNER IS . . . ?

Clearly animals have amazing brains. They have developed different brain abilities to help them live and thrive in a variety of environments and circumstances. Brains that solve problems. Brains that retain memories. Brains that make plans. Brains that communicate. Brains that create tools. Brains that learn quickly. Brains that are spread throughout the body.

But the question remains: who has the most marvelous mind of them all?

Here's a reminder of the challengers:

THE BRAINY BLABBERMOUTH A.K.A.
THE AFRICAN GREY PARROT

THE INTELLIGENT IMPOSTER A.K.A.
THE *PORTIA* JUMPING SPIDER

THE PLAYFUL PLANNER A.K.A.
THE BOTTLENOSE DOLPHIN

THE ASTUTE ANALYZER A.K.A.
THE RAT

THE MAGNIFICENT MEMORIZER A.K.A.
THE ELEPHANT

THE CLEVER COMPANION A.K.A.
THE DOMESTIC DOG

THE SENSIBLE SOLVER A.K.A.
THE COMMON RAVEN

THE MANY-HANDED MASTERMIND A.K.A.
THE OCTOPUS

THE LIVELY LEARNER A.K.A.
THE PIG

THE TALENTED TOOLMAKER A.K.A.
THE CHIMPANZEE

You rated them as you read, and now you get to pick a single winner.

Do you pick the most useful brainpower? The weirdest? The brainpower most similar to ours?

Or maybe you pick the one that makes you laugh the most?

It's up to you.

You now have the sacred duty of crowning the winner of the Coolest Cranium.

GLOSSARY

Agitated: to feel upset, disturbed, or anxious

Anvil: a heavy block with a flat top where objects are hammered

Camouflage: to hide or disguise something so it looks like its surroundings

Matriarch: a female who rules a family or group, especially a mother who is the head of the family

Navigator: a person who plans or finds the route to a place

Neurons: the nerve cells that carry electrical signals throughout the body

Pachyderm: an outdated word used to describe elephants

Palps: little leg-like appendages near the mouth of spiders and other arthropods
used for grasping and sensing

Predator: an animal that gets its food by hunting or killing other animals

Prey: an animal that is hunted or killed to be food for another animal

Sediment: solid material (like sand, rocks, minerals, and the remains of plants and animals)
that settles at the bottom of a liquid

Vertebrates: animals with a spinal cord surrounded by backbone,
such as mammals, birds, amphibians, reptiles, and fish

For the bibliography, further reading, and other activities,
please visit **WWW.JOCELYNRISH.COM.**